Judoon Afternoon

Written by Trevor Baxendale

Based on the television script
"Prisoner of the Judoon" by Phil Ford

Contents

Chapter	Page
1 Sarah Jane's Secret	2
2 Captain Tybo's Mission	6
3 After That Alien!	11
4 Androvax's Spaceship	16

Chapter 1
Sarah Jane's Secret

Sarah Jane Smith lives at 13 Bannerman Road. It's an old house in a quiet road...and inside the attic, there is a fantastic secret!

The secret is an amazing computer called Mr Smith. He can think and talk! He helps Sarah Jane with her secret job – saving Earth from alien invaders.

Luke is Sarah Jane's son. Luke and his friends, Clyde and Rani, help Sarah Jane, too.

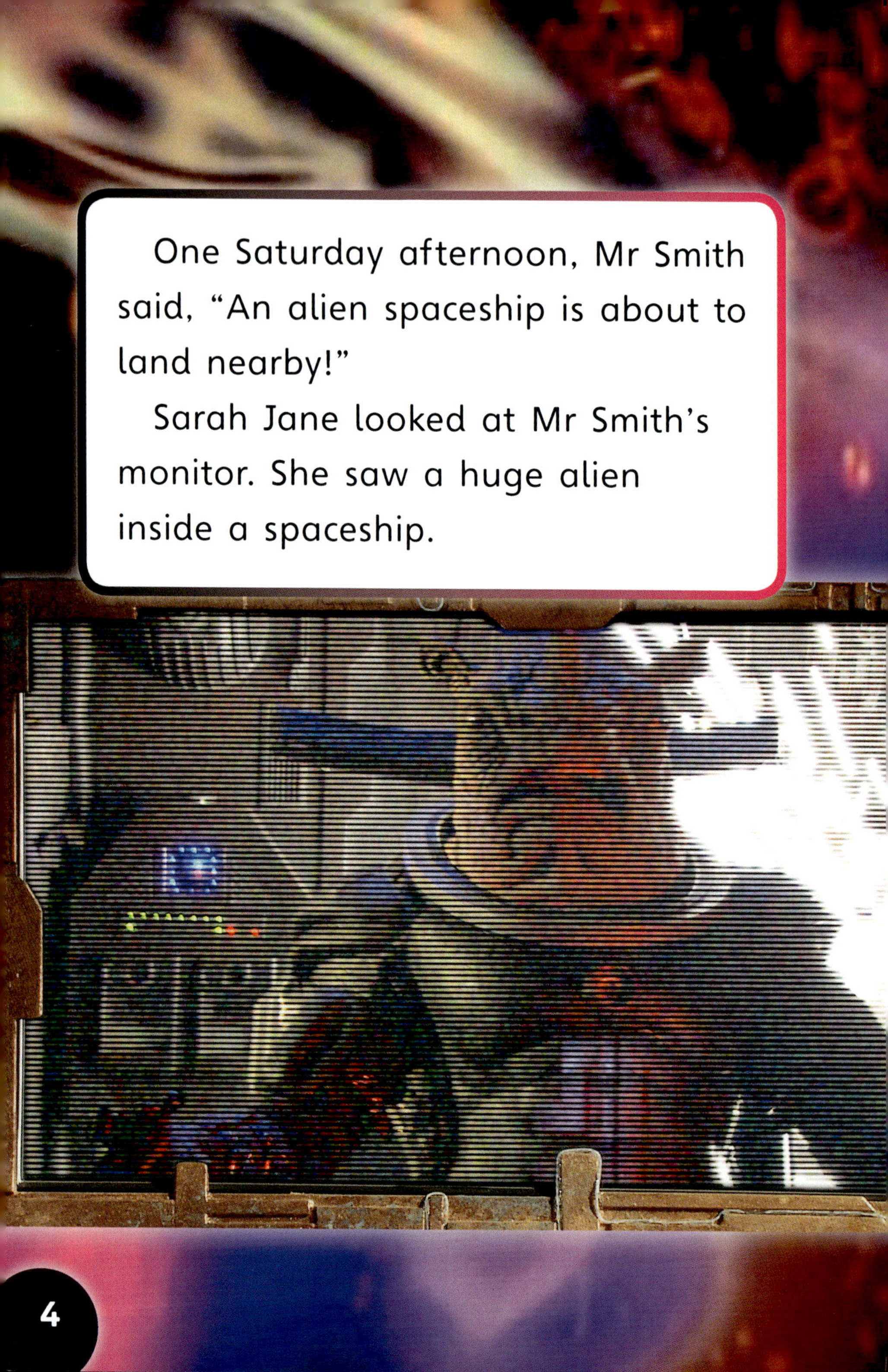

One Saturday afternoon, Mr Smith said, "An alien spaceship is about to land nearby!"

Sarah Jane looked at Mr Smith's monitor. She saw a huge alien inside a spaceship.

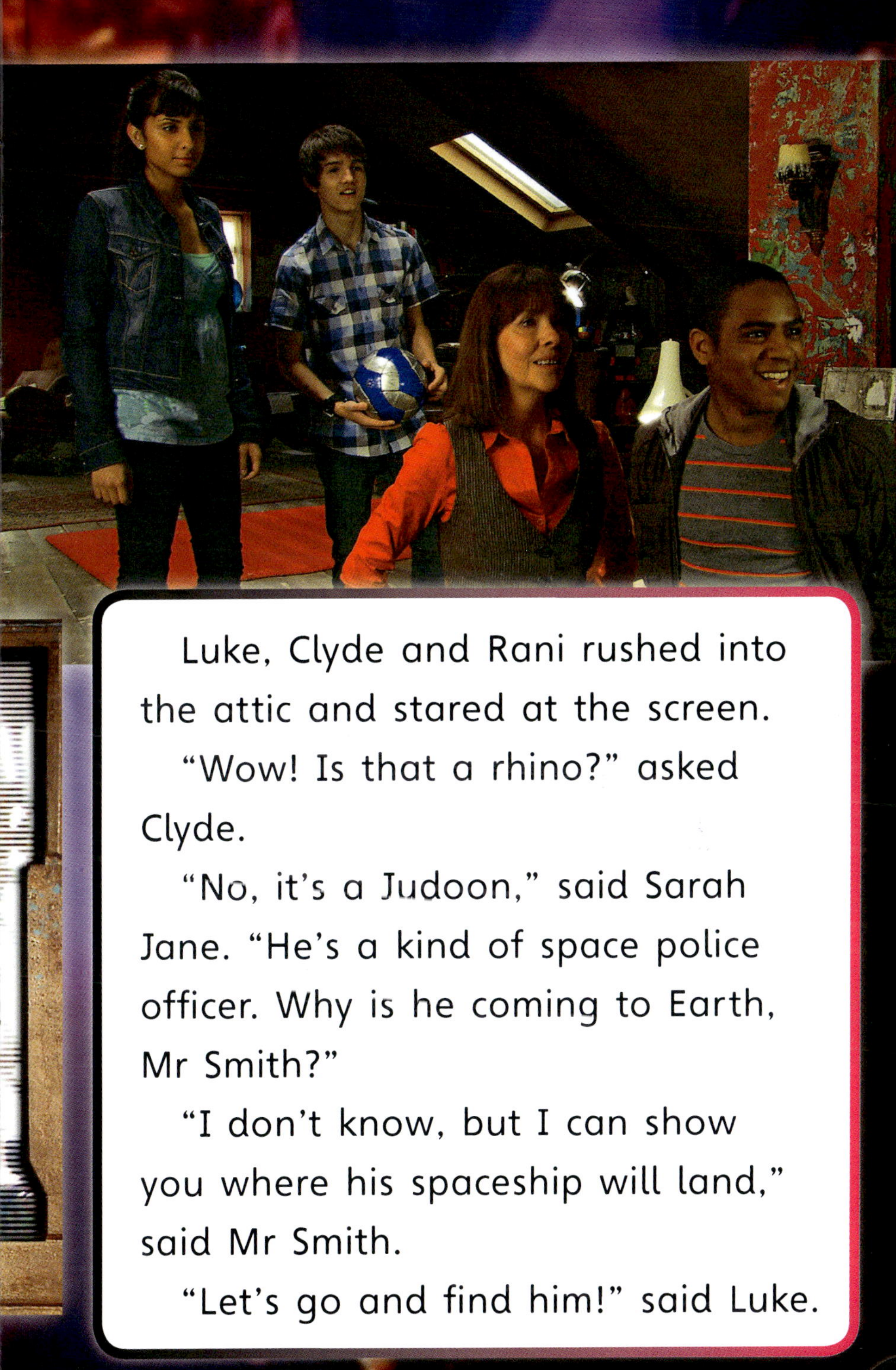

Luke, Clyde and Rani rushed into the attic and stared at the screen.

"Wow! Is that a rhino?" asked Clyde.

"No, it's a Judoon," said Sarah Jane. "He's a kind of space police officer. Why is he coming to Earth, Mr Smith?"

"I don't know, but I can show you where his spaceship will land," said Mr Smith.

"Let's go and find him!" said Luke.

Chapter 2
Captain Tybo's Mission

The spaceship landed on an empty street not far from Sarah Jane's house. Sarah Jane, Luke, Clyde and Rani raced to the street to look for the Judoon.

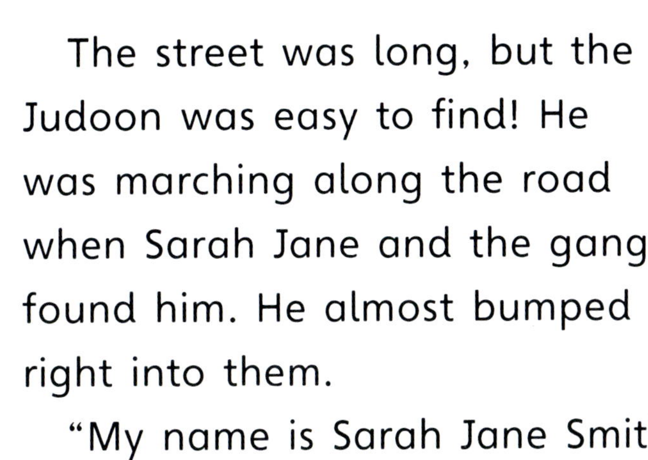

The street was long, but the Judoon was easy to find! He was marching along the road when Sarah Jane and the gang found him. He almost bumped right into them.

"My name is Sarah Jane Smith," said Sarah Jane to the Judoon.

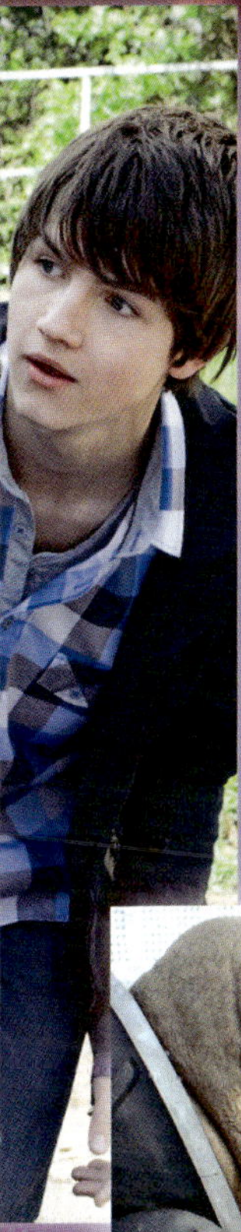

"I am Judoon Captain Tybo," the alien said in a deep voice. "I am chasing an alien called Androvax. He wants to destroy Earth. I have been sent to arrest him before he can do any harm."

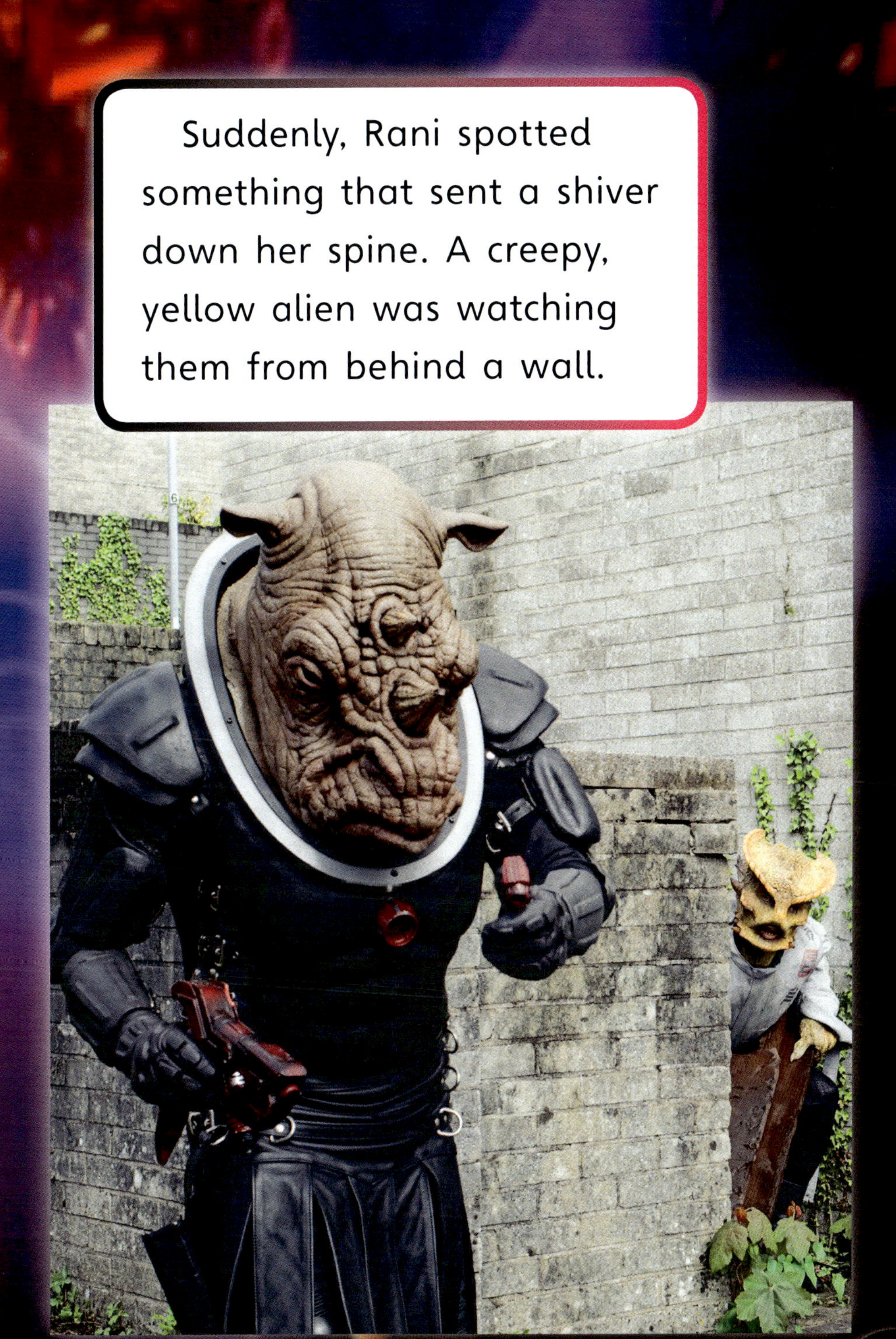

Suddenly, Rani spotted something that sent a shiver down her spine. A creepy, yellow alien was watching them from behind a wall.

"Look out!" shouted Rani. "There he is!"

Androvax heard Rani's shout and raced away down the path. Captain Tybo and the gang chased after him.

Chapter 3
After That Alien!

Androvax was very fast and Captain Tybo could not keep up with him.

"We need a car," said Clyde.

Captain Tybo spotted a police car with two police officers inside. It was just the thing to help them catch Androvax!

Captain Tybo held up his hand to stop the car, and it skidded to a stop in front of him.

"I am a space police officer," said Tybo. "I need to borrow your car."

The police officers were scared. They nodded, jumped out of the car and ran away as fast as they could!

Captain Tybo and the others got into the police car. They were soon chasing after Androvax at top speed.

Androvax saw them coming in the police car. He raced back towards his spaceship so he could escape.

Chapter 4
Androvax's Spaceship

The tyres screeched as Tybo stopped the car. Everyone jumped out just as Androvax reached his spaceship.

Captain Tybo did not want to let Androvax escape now.

"Androvax! You are under arrest!" he boomed.

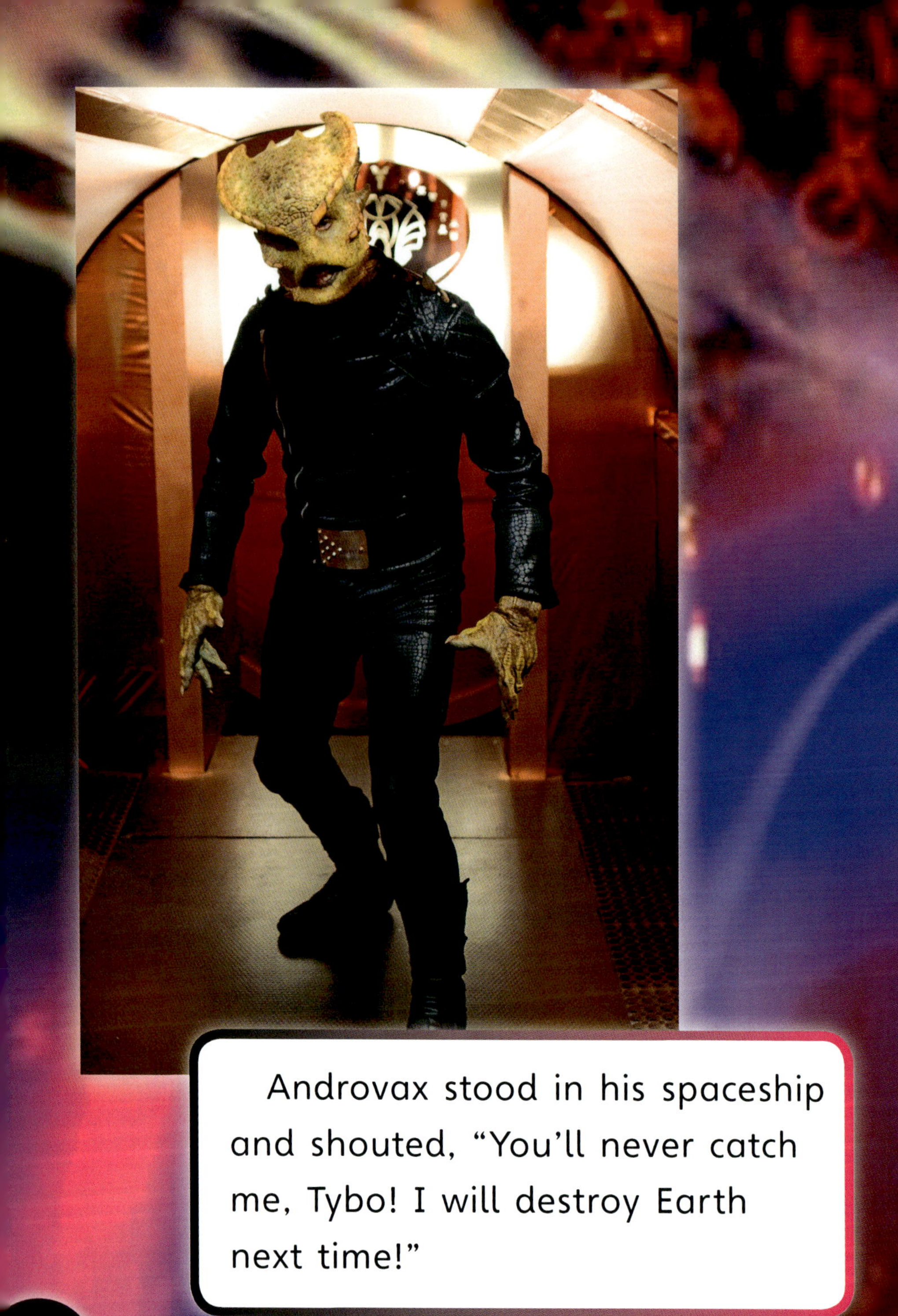

Androvax stood in his spaceship and shouted, “You’ll never catch me, Tybo! I will destroy Earth next time!”

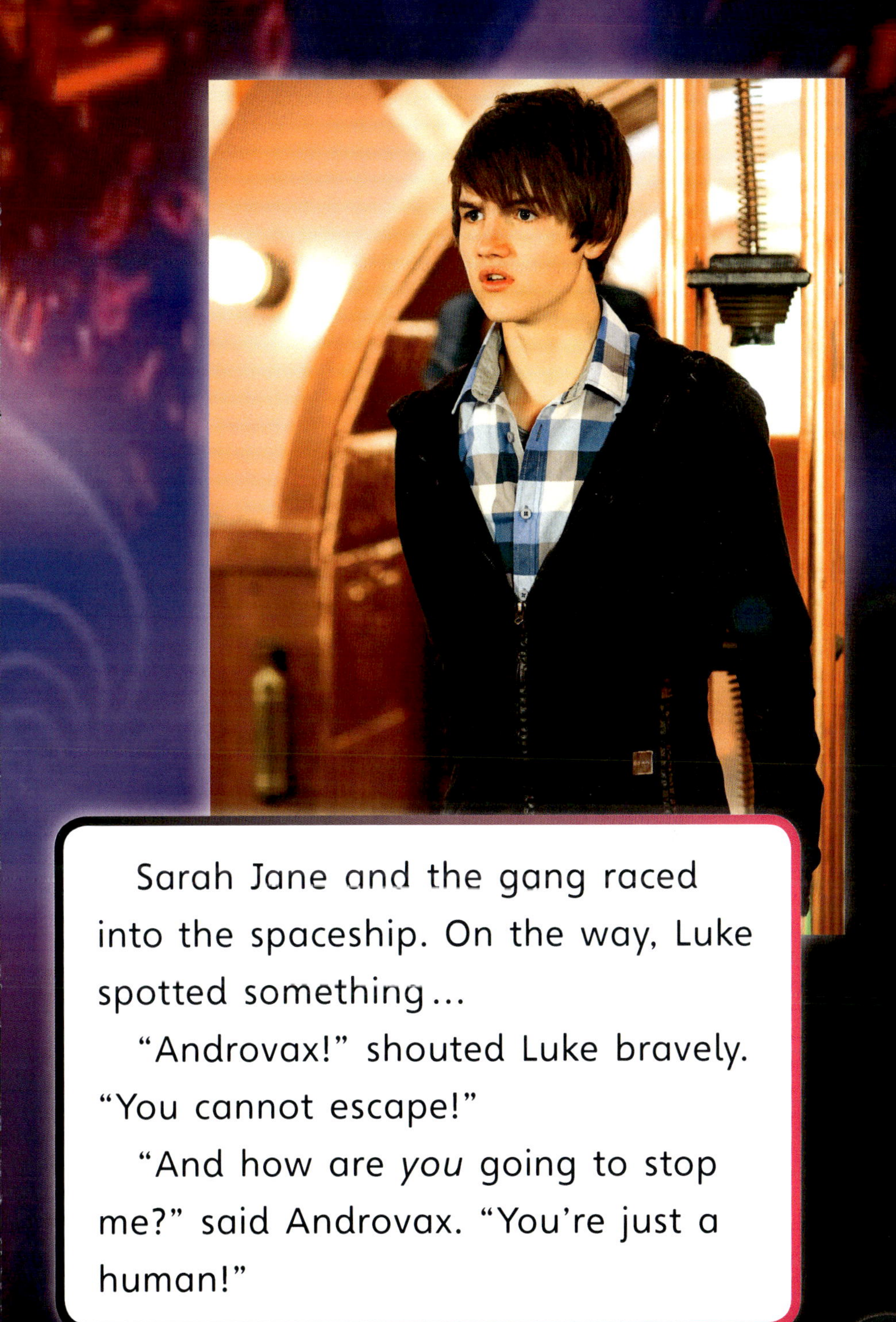

Sarah Jane and the gang raced into the spaceship. On the way, Luke spotted something...

"Androvax!" shouted Luke bravely. "You cannot escape!"

"And how are *you* going to stop me?" said Androvax. "You're just a human!"

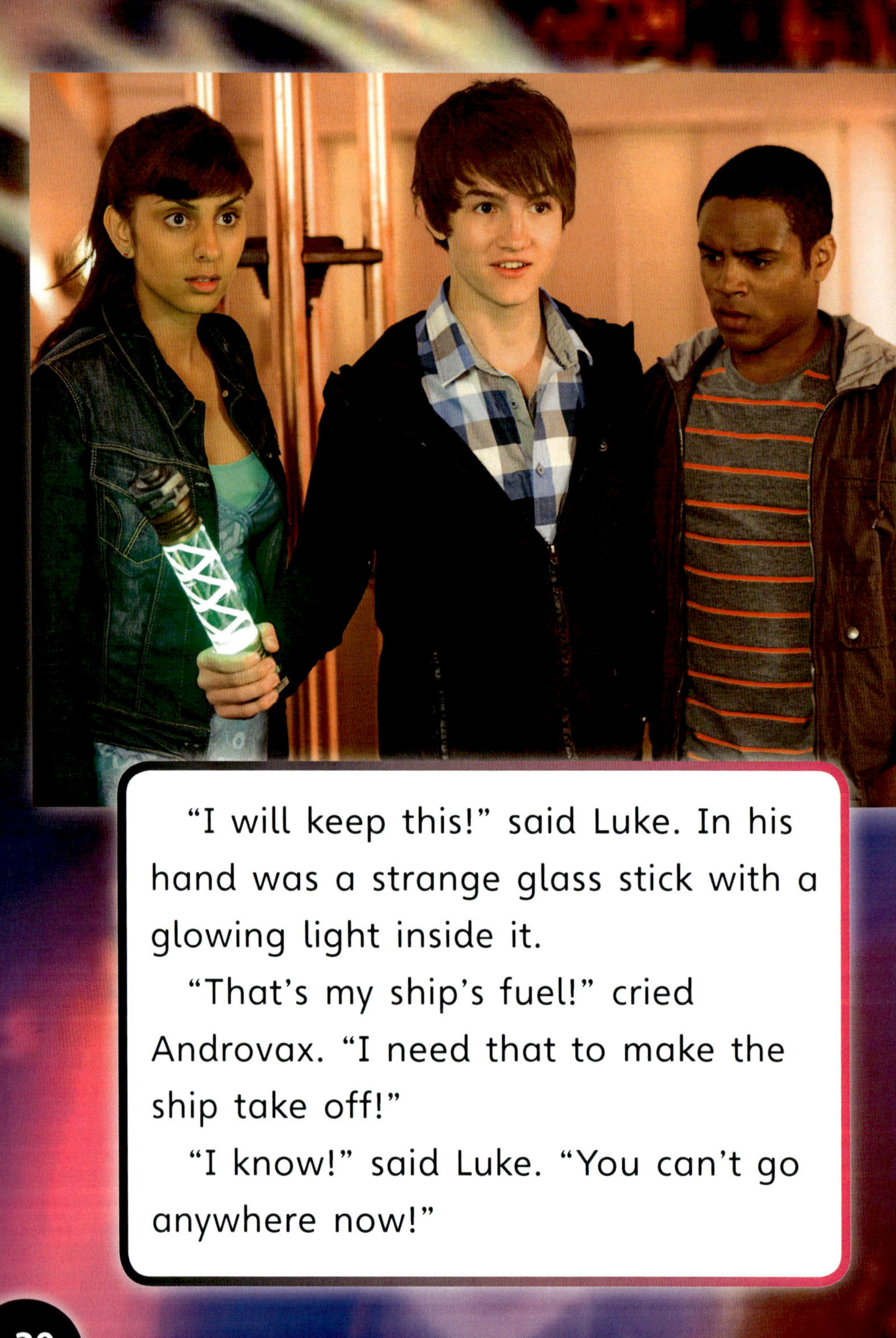

"I will keep this!" said Luke. In his hand was a strange glass stick with a glowing light inside it.

"That's my ship's fuel!" cried Androvax. "I need that to make the ship take off!"

"I know!" said Luke. "You can't go anywhere now!"

"You will never escape again!" agreed Captain Tybo. He put handcuffs on Androvax's wrists.

Androvax was not happy at all. "It's bad enough being caught by a Judoon," he said, "but by humans...!"

“Be quiet!” Captain Tybo said. He turned to Sarah Jane and the gang and thanked them. “You were very helpful – for humans,” he said.

When Sarah Jane, Luke, Clyde and Rani were safely back outside, Tybo flew off in Androvax's spaceship. He took Androvax to prison on a distant planet, far away from Earth.

“Thank goodness that’s over,” said Sarah Jane as they watched the spaceship leave. “We don’t want any more afternoons like this one!”